# On Roll the Days

Susan-Gaye Anderson
# On Roll the Days

*On Roll the Days*
ISBN 978 1 76041 851 9
Copyright © text Susan-Gaye Anderson 2020
Cover photo by Mahir Uysal on Unsplash

First published 2020 by
**Ginninderra Press**
PO Box 3461 Port Adelaide 5015 Australia
www.ginninderrapress.com.au

# Contents

| | |
|---|---|
| Belonging | 7 |
| In the Gallery | 8 |
| Haunted | 9 |
| A Koori Cry | 10 |
| A Ballad | 11 |
| Which One is the Play | 12 |
| Aunt Maude | 13 |
| Destination | 14 |
| He Never Really Liked Me | 15 |
| Aunt Girlie | 16 |
| There I Am | 18 |
| Trembling Hand | 19 |
| Scarlet Fingers | 20 |
| A Blob | 21 |
| Little Bug | 22 |
| Rain on the Windowpane | 23 |
| The Shadow | 25 |
| On Roll the Days | 26 |
| The Shed | 28 |
| Down the Street | 29 |
| Requiem | 30 |
| Home Again | 31 |
| Maps | 33 |
| Amelia | 34 |
| Jack of All Trades | 35 |
| Five O'clock and Ginger Rogers | 36 |
| About the Author | 37 |

# Belonging

I am a stranger here
alien amongst harsh dry leaves cracking underfoot
on earth scarred by thirst
above me flapping wings gain height
a sheet of white dips and weaves in a cruel sky
then plummets down
shrieks of terror rip apart that false quiet

Trees crowd me
leaves hang lifeless like old hands
trembling waiting for a breeze
to drift away

I knew a place once
where bare feet trod so lightly
only scurrying crabs knew they were there
the sea rose swelling forward
then drew back
then began again lapping and lulling
on pale sand constant and timeless

I belonged there.

# In the Gallery

I stand quite still in this vast quiet space,
hearing nothing but my breathing,
only a smatter of muffled conversation
subdued, respectful, from a nearby room.

I stare at the painting on the wall,
at the splashes of mad, wild colour.

Did the artist stand back, then rush towards
the canvas with frantic jabs of dripping paint?

I can't look away I'm drowning in this art.
I refuse to read the written text beside the work.
I don't need an explanation, a clear narrative.

Here I am in another realm away from the banal
and been given a rush of pure joy, that is enough.

# Haunted

There are haunting images that remain etched deep in my mind
of an oily sea on which floats a soiled yellow life jacket and a shoe
another of railway tracks weary ragged men women children
trudging beside the line single file their eyes dull with despair
surely leaving behind memories of the most terrible kind
cruelly cast aside by mad greed or fanatic extreme power
is this a journey to indifferent safety or to lonely isolation
will they be ignored by those who do not want anyone
will not have anyone fracture their complacent lives

# A Koori Cry

Stand tall my son stand tall
They've got you against the wall
Each will load his gun
Aiming them every one

You once had a choice to be
A spirit wild and free
You went against the stream
Followed your inherent dream

Stand tall my son stand tall
They've got you against the wall
Each will load his gun
Aiming at everyone

They locked you inside
Narrowed your boundaries wide
Smiled and told you lies
Never listened to your cries

Stand tall my son stand tall
They've got you against the wall
Each will load his gun
Aiming at everyone.

# A Ballad

Where did they go to those babes of mine
They were there for a moment
Such a short time
I bathed fed them walked the floor
Looked up for a second
They were out of the door

Where did they go to those babes of mine
They were there for a moment
Such a short time
I washed clothed and cleaned
They kept me poor
Then they weren't there any more.

Where did they go to those babes of mine
They were there for a moment
Such a short time
I read to them cooked for them
Told them to love to be true to be sure
Then they left for a foreign shore.

Where did they go to those babes of mine
They were there for a moment
Such a short time
They left me sadder but wiser
Knowing the truth
A bird doesn't stay long on the roof.

# Which One is the Play

There seems a sense of theatre in each day
We don disguises then wait for praise
Give what is needed as we act our play
Vainly claiming attention with fawning ways
Spend our lives demanding to be heard
Feign tears and laughter with studied ease
In parody of others mock their words
Rehearsing speeches with intent to please
We hide behind costumes the face a mask
Speak other's words to hide our own
Quick glib answers to questions asked
Heroes lovers clowns then retreat alone.

Illusion merged with real life is a way
To prevent us asking which one is the play.

# Aunt Maude

Sitting there squeezed between the cushions on the couch
beige and green floral too big for her small sharp frame
her feet planted firmly on the ground knees pressed together
she smooths the crease in her skirt and smiles at me
but not enough to make lines appear around the eyes
we need to talk or are you racing out to meet someone
somehow I get a vision of orgies by a river bank
a picnic rug wine spilled too loud laughter
with her lace-trimmed hanky she dabs at her mouth
then tucks it neatly inside her black handbag
her nervous fingers touch the buttons on her dress
checking all are in place one hand pats her hair
I lay my hand carelessly over the back of my chair
my scarlet fingernails defiant in that stifling room.

# Destination

Now it makes sense sitting in the boat facing backwards
For it certainly is not the destination but the journey
Looking back over the choppy sea a wave wetting my feet
I do not want to see where the bow is pointing
My withered arms spotted with age grip the oars
This is not for the weak this is an endurance test
My gaze is fixed grimly on where I have been
Sees dancing feet under swirling taffeta and net
shining eyes velvet skin music and lust
Oh that gorgeous word how it makes me smile
But the distance from the shore is growing immense
This takes strength and courage to row on.

# He Never Really Liked Me

It came to me quite suddenly sitting there at the breakfast table
with toast crumbs and plates greasy with curled up bits of bacon
I don't think he ever really liked me I'm not sure he ever did
he in his pale grey three-piece suit and nicotine-stained fingers
he was always first with the witty lines the quick barbs
funny but teetering just on the edge of cruelty
what an audience he had holding forth one hand on his hip
how all of us laughed too quickly at times
he was the first to wear a bow tie the kind you tie yourself
showy the others copied but they never wore it as well
he wrote a brilliant thesis we all went out to celebrate
drinking cheap red wine in a courtyard covered with vines
he stood on a chair and did a clever imitation of us all
later on the way home I wondered why he mocked us so
it was a surprise when he asked me to go away for a weekend
he always seemed to look away before I finished a sentence
in the French restaurant I caught a look between him and the waiter
as I stumbled over my order I was never good at French
we got married in July the day was sullen with a threat of rain
on the way to the church I picked at the petals on my bouquet
and asked the driver to go around the block once again
as I walked down the aisle I saw him standing there looking at his watch
I don't think he ever really liked me I'm not sure he ever did
he in is his pale grey three-piece suit and nicotine-stained fingers.

# Aunt Girlie

She wore her hair rolled over an old stocking.
Around her neck swayed a necklace of amber beads
That caught the light like chunks of toffee.
I loved the smell of her, eau de cologne and peppermints
Which she kept in a round blue tin in a shiny black handbag
That closed with a loud clunk.
Her stockings sagged loose and her spindly legs
Felt frail when I sat on her knee and played
With the fine silver bracelets she wore on her arm
Twelve, I counted them every time.

I sat on the end of her bed hugging my knees
While she showed me faded brown photographs
Of young men in khaki.
She told me I had the family hands,
They were a gift and each night before sleep
I must rub them with glycerine.

I stayed in her weatherboard cottage
Where jasmine climbed over the peeling paint
On a picket fence with a gate that creaked.
We fed sparrows with crumbs of white bread
On the springy back lawn under a clothesline
With fat wooden pegs.

In the mornings when the grass was wet with dew
I would hear her footsteps on the wooden floor
And leap out of bed, squeeze into my slippers
With my pyjamas flapping, run down the hall.
There she would be with her grey hair down
Milk bottle in her hand, still in a dressing gown
The cat rubbing against her ankles purring loud.

She was my father's favourite sister
And when she died I locked myself in my room
And cried and cried and cried.

# There I Am

You push squeeze pummel and pinch
You crack crease smother and hover
I have no room to breathe

I need a cushion of space
Where I cannot be found
A solace a shelter a quiet place

I have given yes on my terms
Was there another way
Not what was wanted you say

You had choices none for me
Right wrong black white
For you clear as can be

There I am see me over there
Looking out at the foliage
Or are the trees bare

Don't walk away words lost
Your head averted
As you pass me by

See the dog dying on the road
Look at his eyes
Then look at me.

# Trembling Hand

In Camberwell where houses are hid
behind neat privet hedges
where ruby glass gleams
down on to crimson Persian rugs
and shiny polished floors
where long curved driveways
hug sleek smug cars
where peony roses grow amid
lupins and lavender
because that's what Edna Walling did
a woman sits staring at the wall
a drink in her trembling hand.

In Collingwood where houses crowd
on to streets that block the light
where windows are broken blinds torn
and dusty bushes struggle to find
enough dirt to survive
where a runt of a dog sniffs the lid
of a rubbish bin pushing it on its side
where slashed on a rusty tin fence
in black paint is written
No Fucking Nukes in this Land
a woman sits staring at the wall
a drink in her trembling hand.

# Scarlet Fingers

I don't want to go down there
Where searing heat shrivels my hair
Engulfs my bones tears at my flesh
Where scarlet fingers lick at my soul
In that soot-black Stygian hole.

I don't want to go down there
Where a crazed spectre crawls in his lair
Stoking monstrous flames of cruelty and pain
Blistering hissing crackles that explode
Into oblivion in that furious damned abode.

I'm afraid to go down there
Grimly challenged by a ghastly stare
To atone for weakness evil and greed
I may grovel lie or betray my friends

Shrieking spare me from time without end.
I don't want to go down there
Where searing heat shrivels my hair
Engulfs my bones tears at my flesh
Where scarlet fingers lick at my soul
In that soot-black Stygian hole.

# A Blob

Clamped sucked to a wall

A blob of black

Waiting to plunder

Fat with obscenity

My flung newspaper misses

Lifts you droning around

I steal close

Pause and whack

You plummet and fall

Oozing stain on my white floor

# Little Bug

Poor frail little bug
        labouring over
                soaring mountains
                        of jagged grass

                      then dropping down

                  a bottomless crater
          recovering then
    grimly heaving
                towards a tiny
                        morsel of food
              spindly legs toiling
        feelers warning
steadfast and brave

but too paltry for a name.

# Rain on the Windowpane

PLINK
PLINK
PLINK
PLINK

Rain on the windowpane
Perched on a chair
Looking out
A child trapped by blame

Did he do it
Break the cup
Frills and ribbons
She wouldn't own up

Snakes and tigers
In jungles lush green
He slashed with his sword
Enemies unseen

One-eared rabbit only friend
When it fell to the ground
Held his hand tight
As they shook at the sound

Sent upstairs
Locked in his room
Rabbit and he
Alone in the gloom

PLINK
PLINK
PLINK
PLINK

Rain on the windowpane

# The Shadow

Her pants sag below her floral printed cotton skirt
The T-shirt has a stain from the flowers she picked
One chubby leg has a Band-Aid over the knee
She clutches in one hand a doll
With glassy blue eyes and ragged hair
She stands on the step near the back door
But can't go in because the shadow will get her
Grab her jump on top of her scratch her skin
So she waits because soon their dog
Will return from exploring bounding leaping
He will bark loudly jump up and down
Growl showing his black lips and pointy teeth
Save her from the monster lurking behind the door
And her mother will turn on the light hugging her
Then the shadow will disappear.

# On Roll the Days

Dearest child innocent hand in mine
I wish I could pause this moment in time

stop the world from joy and pain
I see you high on my shoulder one bright day
dazzled eyes shining with all you can see
ducks on the lake leaves in the tree

upside down looped over the monkey bar
limbs supple hair fanning the ground
a gap in your teeth as you grin at me

alone with your secrets door closed
staring at a mirror free of clothes
or writing in a book with a lock and key

twisting and turning on roll the days
now you have learned devious ways
you preen flirt make false promises of love

in time older treasuring moments of solitude
seeking reason while asserting your place
you find books and music an escape

youth gone accountable a child of your own
old promises forgotten dreams flown
until finally slow forgetful with age

eyes clouded weary from all you have seen
talking to others only of what has been
I see all this while your hand clasps mine

Some need twists your face your voice a whine
You tug at my sleeve an urgent demand
Ah child too late you have begun.

# The Shed

I did out the shed on Sunday
While the rain dribbled down
And the dog lay snoring at my feet
I found paint tins with romantic names
Moonlight Misty Morning Sundown
A suitcase the lock rusted and inside
Paper patterns of fancy dress costumes
A fairy with a tinsel halo a pirate a clown
A bike leant against the wall tyres flat
It was warm inside the shed
I looked through a spiral of cobwebs
While outside the rain slid down
On a shelf was a battered school bag
A gold insignia *Ora et Labora*
Inside a torn lined exercise book
Round looped writing 'My Holiday'
On the floor lay a yellow newspaper
Headlines screaming Whitlam Out!
Nearby were football boots clogged with mud
One lace broken the other lace gone
The rain made heavy the leaves on the vine
Yellow flowers that grew over the door
A branch scraped against the window
The dog stirred looked at me and sighed.

# Down the Street

We pad down the street my dog and I
Under a sky of purple blue
Pin pricks of delicate light
And a sliver of moon floats by.

We pad down the street my dog and I
On pavement still warm from the day
He lopes along tail wagging by my side
Lifts an ear when he hears me say stay!

We pad down the street my dog and I
Seeing houses lit from within
A parade of interrupted scenes
A woman bending over a rubbish bin

We pad down the street my dog and I
A face at a window a man in a dressing gown
One arm raised as though in greeting
Before the blind slides down.

We pad down the street my dog and I
A violin makes the sweetest sound
We stumble over broken concrete
On rubble near a building mound.

We pad down the street my dog and I
A fallen bike a forgotten shoe
A sprinkler spraying the manicured lawn
The sky turns dark a grey black hue.

We pad down the street my dog and I
The road ends I feel suddenly alone
My dog looks at me I smile
and we head for home.

# Requiem

From afar the muffled drone of cars
A tap drips a sombre rhythm
A bird sits mute on a bough
Staring gravely
On the sill gloves lie encrusted with earth
Abandoned the fingers curled
Inside a door closes with a sigh
In this room sheets on the bed thin with age
A watch rests on the table
Hands point to another time
Petals once crimson droop onto lace
Silver frames hold smiling faces
Slatted blinds yield a weak afternoon sun
Shafts of pale light reflect dust
Drifting down
A grey cobweb wafts from the ceiling
Slowly moving encroaching further
A fallen cushion sags in a corner
On shelves layered in rows
Clothing is neatly folded
I will take those
But what will I do
With the perfume you always wore.

# Home Again

The chestnut trees were so green this time
lining those wide boulevards that sweep
down to grand fountains and stone figures
poised untouched by wars and change.
Elegant trees stately and proud
like their city pompous old.
Not like our ragged trees that shed
careless grey brown leaves
from jagged twigs and stringy bark.

I think of their city now I'm not there
I can taste the bitter black coffee
see the red checked table cloths at the café
where waiters run in long starched aprons
tied neatly in front with a bow.
They speak softly there, *Bonjour Madame*
the pitch high then low soft polite
not like our harsh flat nasal drawl.

I found in my pocket a Metro ticket *un billet*
and a paper bag *Magasin pour les Femmes*
I bought gloves for the leaves were turning red
and the wind had grown chill
They cost fifty francs more than I had
I thought I could wear them in winter back home.

G'day, love! Have a great trip been away long?
Brash no respect yet you have to smile.
The space, the air, so fresh, the sky vast
and people who look you right in the eye.

What is it that gets inside
stays in your heart deep in your veins
what is it that makes it so good to be home again?

# Maps

Maps never show people never show faces
looking up in wonder at the night sky
or tending animals driving tractors
waiting desperate for rain to fall
in a land ravaged by savage drought
forests are marked with green but you can't hear
the sound of the wind whispering through the pines
borders are marked by thick lines dividing those
who pray to another God speak in different tongues
who huddle together in front of an open fire
or toss on humid nights in sheets bathed in sweat.
rivers with grand names run nourishing through towns
while children leap into the water in innocent delight
maps are remote cold clinical with facts and figures
never revealing courage fear and the truth of living.

# Amelia

Falling out of the sky a great mass of metal
Hurtling down into a sea the colour of stale blood
The wind shaking the palm fronds in a death rattle
Rats crouching waiting in dense mangrove swamps
One wing points to the sky above
The other like a finger to the sea below
Tearing screaming through the dense clouds
Plummeting down with deadly precision
Through the shocked air
Forcing waves to part explode
Into a vortex of foam and steel
A dreadful sound then more ghastly
Nothing.
Silence.
The sea swallows all hope.

# Jack of All Trades

She pouts her lips at me
'Oh you're so good at that
doing so many different things.'
Yes that's me darting here and there
shimmying from this to that.
Running out the door
to where and why?
Never still never composed
never measured never planned.
Others, oh the research!
The libraries the PhDs
the meticulous serious projects
with letters after their names.

I knit cactus make felt books
write shallow frivolous poems.
One day my body of work
will end up in a shredder
or at the local op shop.

# Five O'clock and Ginger Rogers

The dishes are done
wiped clean
the bench is free of clutter
the floor is swept
the rubbish kept
in a white plastic bucket
the oven is on
zucchini chopped
salad crisp in a bowl
the table is set two spoons and a fork
a knife for bread and butter
serviettes folded
next to the plate
custard cools in the mould
the dog is fed
the radio set
blinds in the room down.

Oh but I long to go dancing!
Spinning and dipping and twirling and swaying
in billowing taffeta and lace.
I would whirl to and fro with a dreamy smile
pearl fingernails glowing brightly
the music would throb as he gazed at me
both arms holding me tightly.

## About the Author

Susan-Gaye Anderson pioneered as a celebrated television presenter in the early days of Australian television, primarily on *The Tarax Show* with GTV 9. During the 1980s, Anderson worked as a professional freelance writer. Her work included feature biographical articles on prominent art professionals for *The Age* newspaper and regular feature articles for *Home Beautiful* magazine. Anderson has since published poetry and short stories in various Australian anthologies. She has had stage plays produced and workshopped in Melbourne and Sydney theatres, including Theatreworks, La Mama, Malthouse, Fortyfivedownstairs Theatre and Griffin Theatre.

www.ingramcontent.com/pod-product-compliance
Lightning Source LLC
Chambersburg PA
CBHW062207100526
44589CB00014B/1996